Advanced

The
Ziggy-Stitch Technique

by Z. Rytka

ISBN 0 9536478 0 3

©1999 by Ziggy Rytka

Author & Publisher Z. Rytka

27 Bowman Place, Halifax, West Yorkshire, HX1 5PD, Tel. 01422 348096

INDEX

Page

1. ....Introduction
2. ....Fast Grab
5. ....Back to front - front to back
7. ....Thread Lock
8. ....Cradle Lock
10. ....Ziggy-Stitch Technique, Figure 1
11. ....Fig 2
12. ....Fig 3
13. ....Fig 4
14. ....Fig 5
15. ....Fig 6
16. ....Fig 7
17. ....Fig 8
18. ....Fig 9
19. ....Fig 10
20. ....Fig 11
21. ....Fig 12
22. ....Fig 13
23. ....Fig 14
24. ....Fig 15
25. ....Fig 16
26. ....Fig 17
27. ....Crossover Parallel
28. ....Kiss Cord

INTRODUCTION

The Ziggy-Stitch is the ability to split apart threads and rejoin them, essentially putting a 'Buttonhole' in the middle of a piece of cord, but it is much much more, the effects and uses that can be made with two bobbins are many and varied.
The technique can also be applied using 3, 4, 5 bobbins to produce 'Spider-Ladder' or 'Diamond-Back' designs.

The Lucet has produced a square sectioned cord of low stretch and high strength for over 1,000 years, from Vikings to Victorians. In 1994 I invented the Lucet Bobbin, designed to carry a skein of thread and to act as a 'Lock' when the Lucet is inactive, since then it has proved itself invaluable in the creation of the Ziggy-Stitch technique which has opened up a whole new world to the Luceter.
In the booklet that follows are step by step instructions on the Ziggy-Stitch Technique with seperate sections for hand and bobbin skills you will need to complete the Ziggy-Stitch, the fast-grab can also be used independently to make straight Lucet cord at high speed, at the back of the booklet I have given instructions on two effects of the Ziggy-Stitch which you can try but there are many more which you can create yourself by changing the length of stitch or distance between, colours, threads, interlocking two Ziggy-Stitched cords or even making Ziggy-Stitches where one side is twice as long as the other creating a 'D' Loop, the choice is yours............Good Luck,

Happy Luceting

H. J. Rytka.

Fast Grab
A high speed method of Luceting.

Wrap the thread through the fingers as illustrated, with an extra turn all the way round the little finger for extra traction.

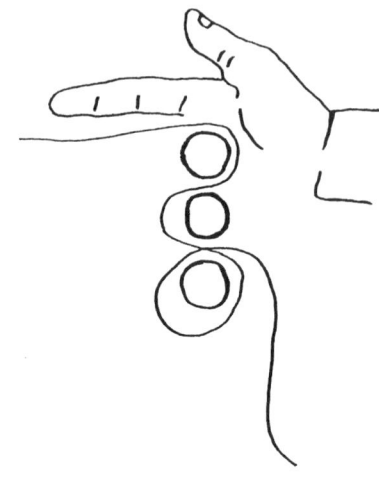

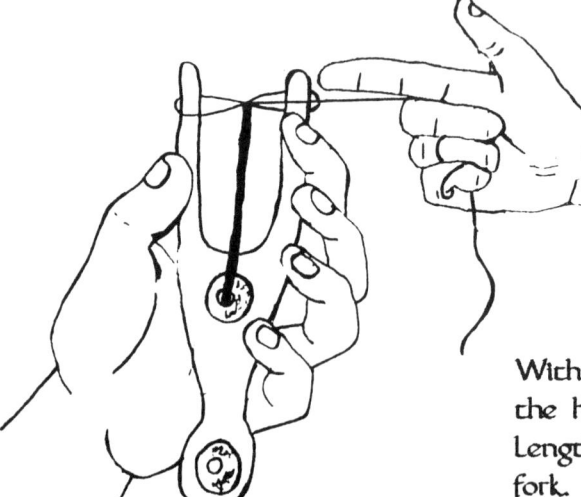

With the working thread taut, the hand should be a fingers length away from the right fork.

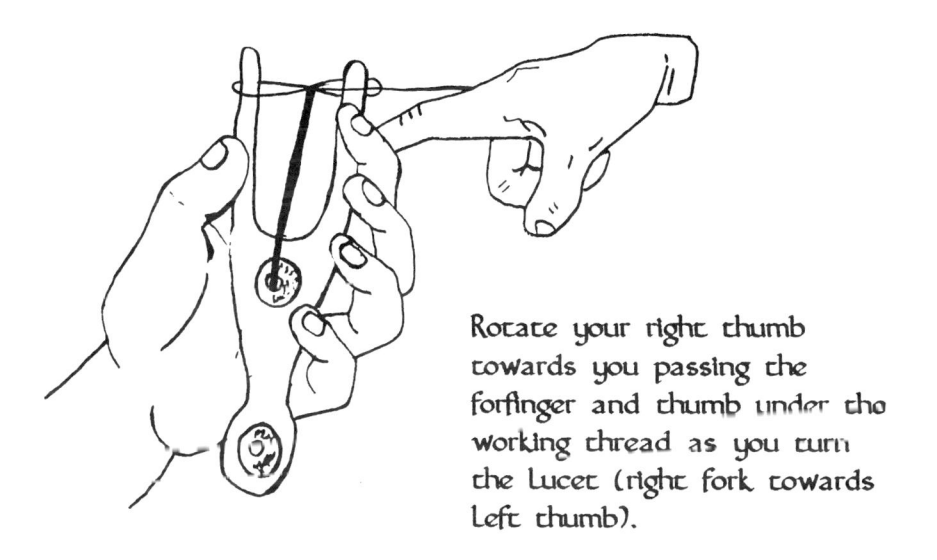

Rotate your right thumb towards you passing the forfinger and thumb under the working thread as you turn the Lucet (right fork towards Left thumb).

TIP As you turn, try not to pull on the working thread, as this will shorten your new right loop

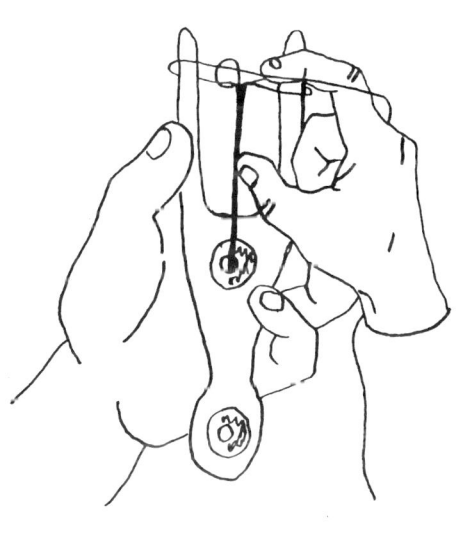

As you turn the Lucet your finger and thumb are reaching for the loop on your new right fork.

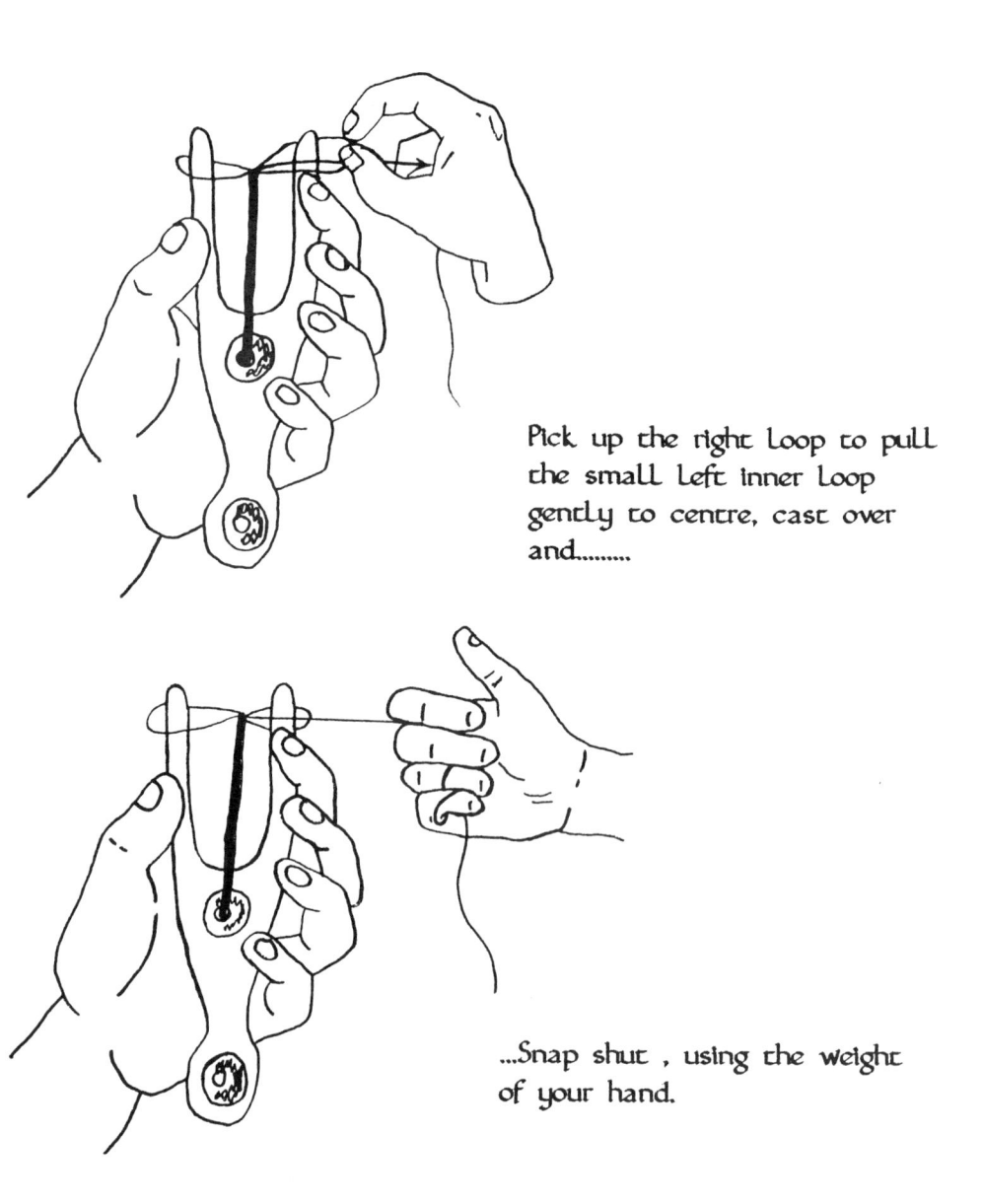

Pick up the right loop to pull the small left inner loop gently to centre, cast over and.........

...Snap shut, using the weight of your hand.

This will bring the finished cord slightly over to the right so that when you turn again you will have a large right loop to pick up and a small one to bring to centre.

Back to Front - Front to Back

This technique is used to control the bobbins in the Ziggy-Stitch. At first stage seperation the thread-locked bobbin (Fig 8) is held by the fingers in the back position. At second stage seperation the cradle-locked bobbin (Fig 12) is held against the lucet in the palm of the hand in the 'front' position.

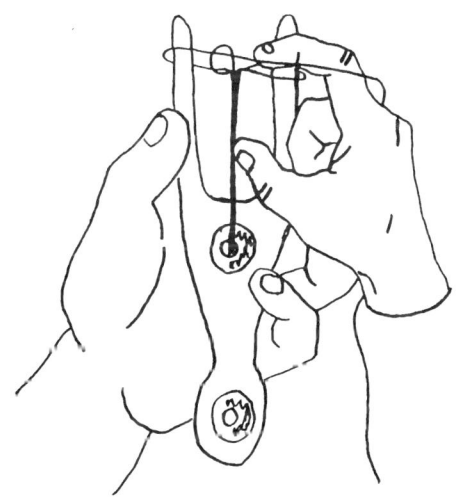

In the 'back' position, pick up, pull to centre, cast and snap shut as in fast grab, then.....

...without altering your grip on the lucet, turn the lucet the opposite way, rotating your left wrist to pass the lucet forks under the working thread and up into the 'front' position.

Pick up, pull to centre, cast and snap shut as usual then turn in the normal direction to the 'back' position, repeat.

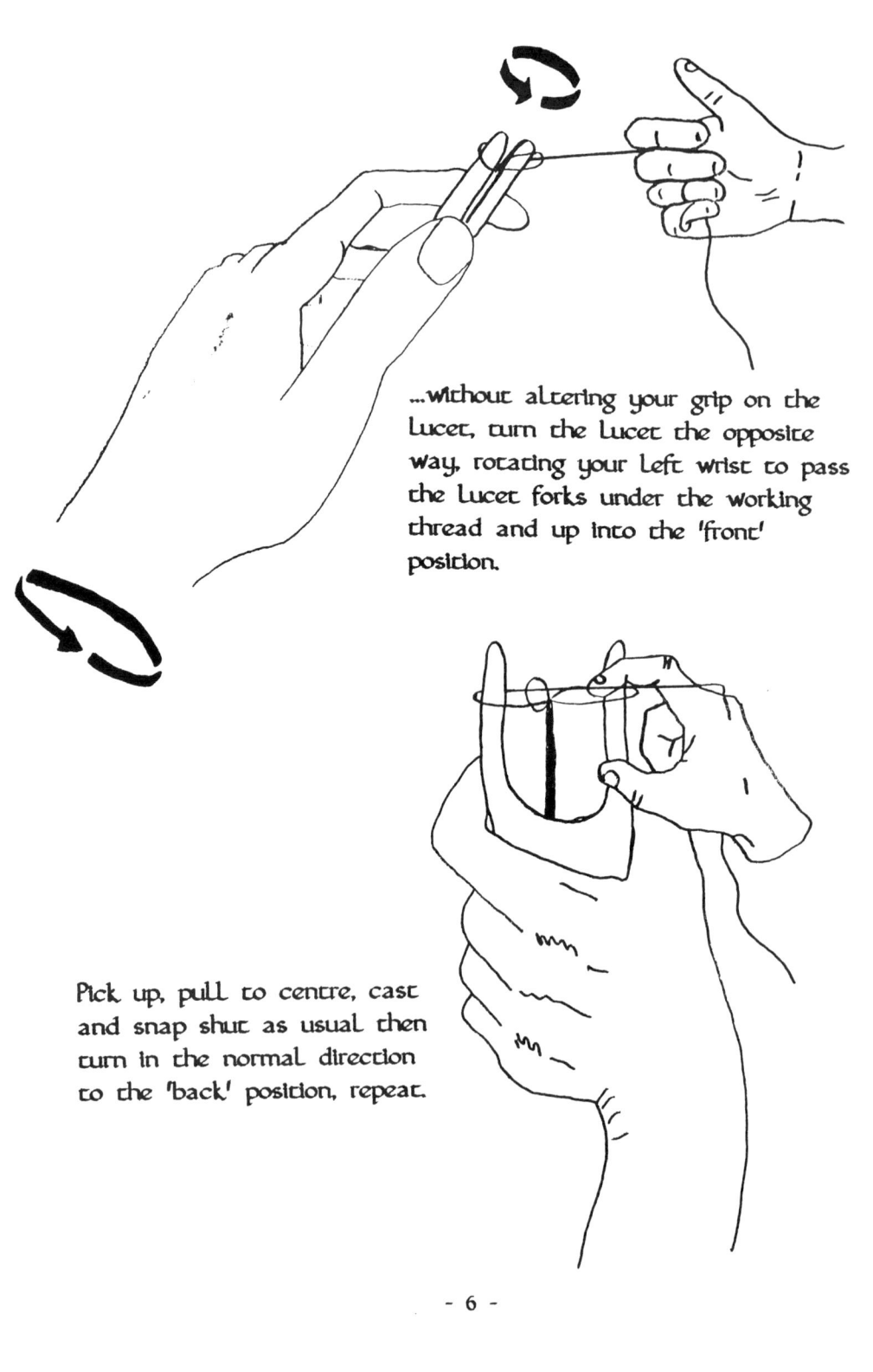

Bobbin techniques

Thread Lock

Pull a loop of thread through the hole using a crochet hook, cast over...

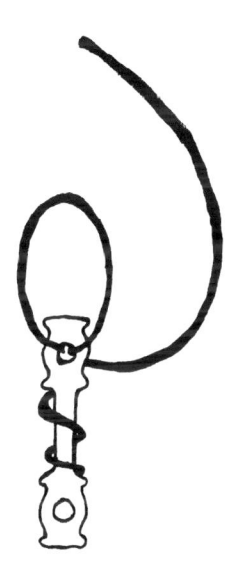

...and pull tight.

Cradle Lock

Lift the left loop off the
lucet using the bobbin

Take hold of the right loop and use
it to pull the left loop close to the
bobbin

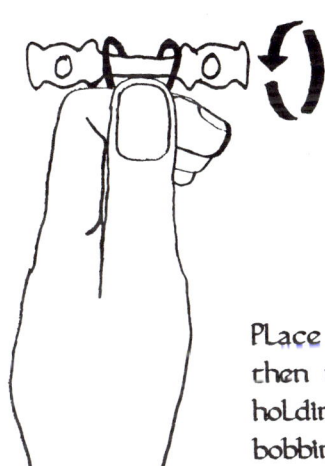

Place the right loop onto the bobbin then rotate the bobbin towards you holding onto the cord close to the bobbin

TIP Make sure the thread is coming from the bottom of the bobbin

To undo the cradle lock rotate in the opposite direction

The Ziggy-Stitch Technique

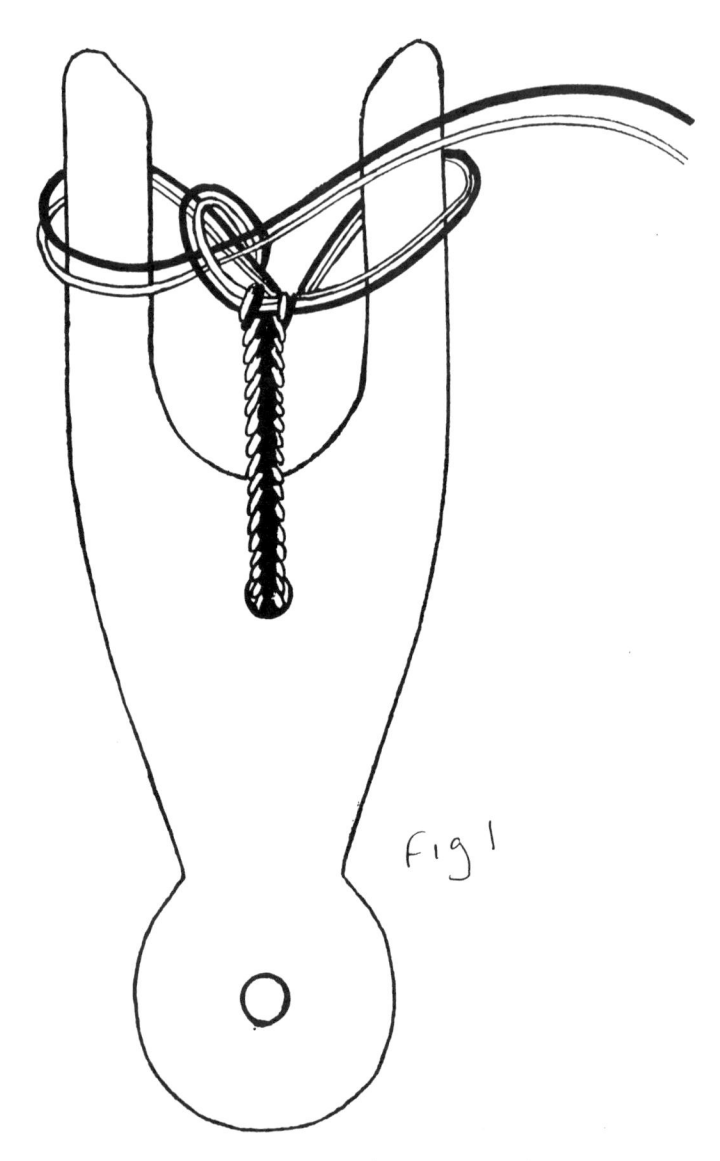

Fig 1

Luceting as normal, pull the bottom loop on the right fork to bring the left inner loop gently to centre, do not cast.

Fig 2

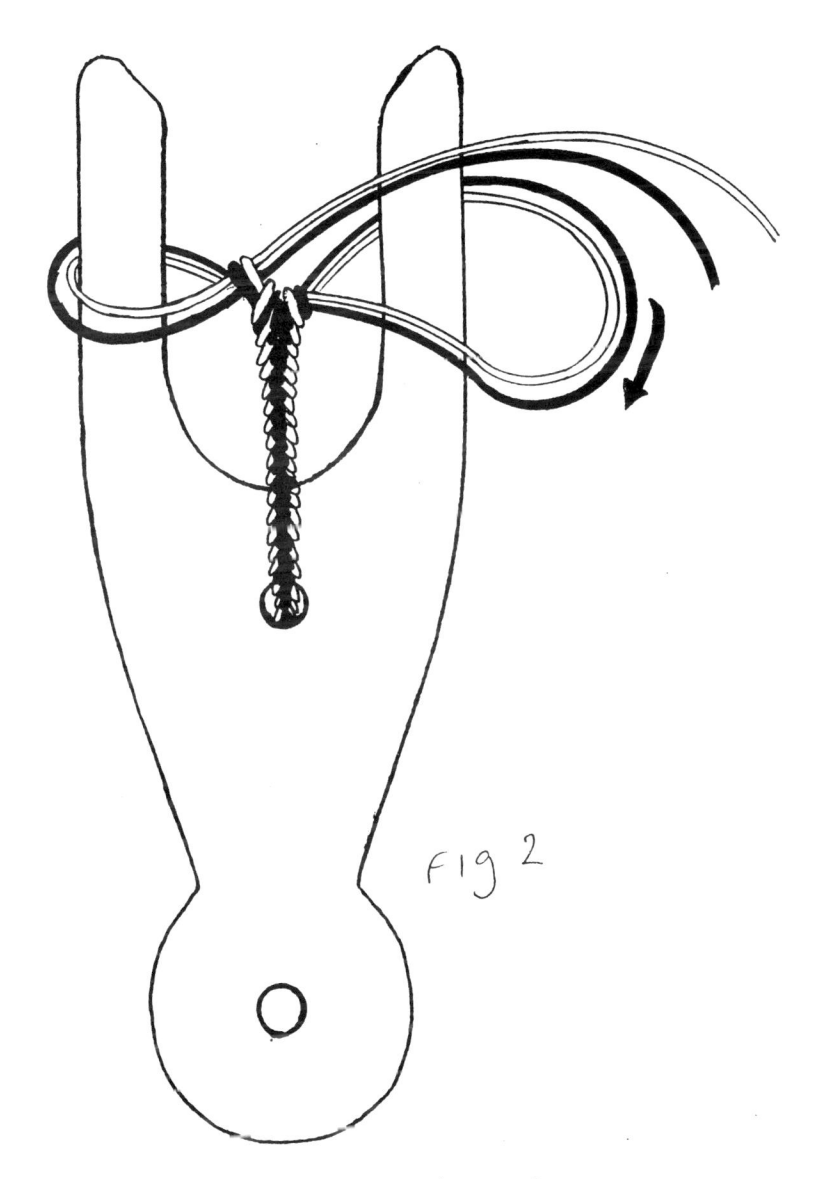

Holding onto the loop, release the working thread tension from your fingers and back-pull the loop away from the right fork, making it larger than usual.

Fig 3

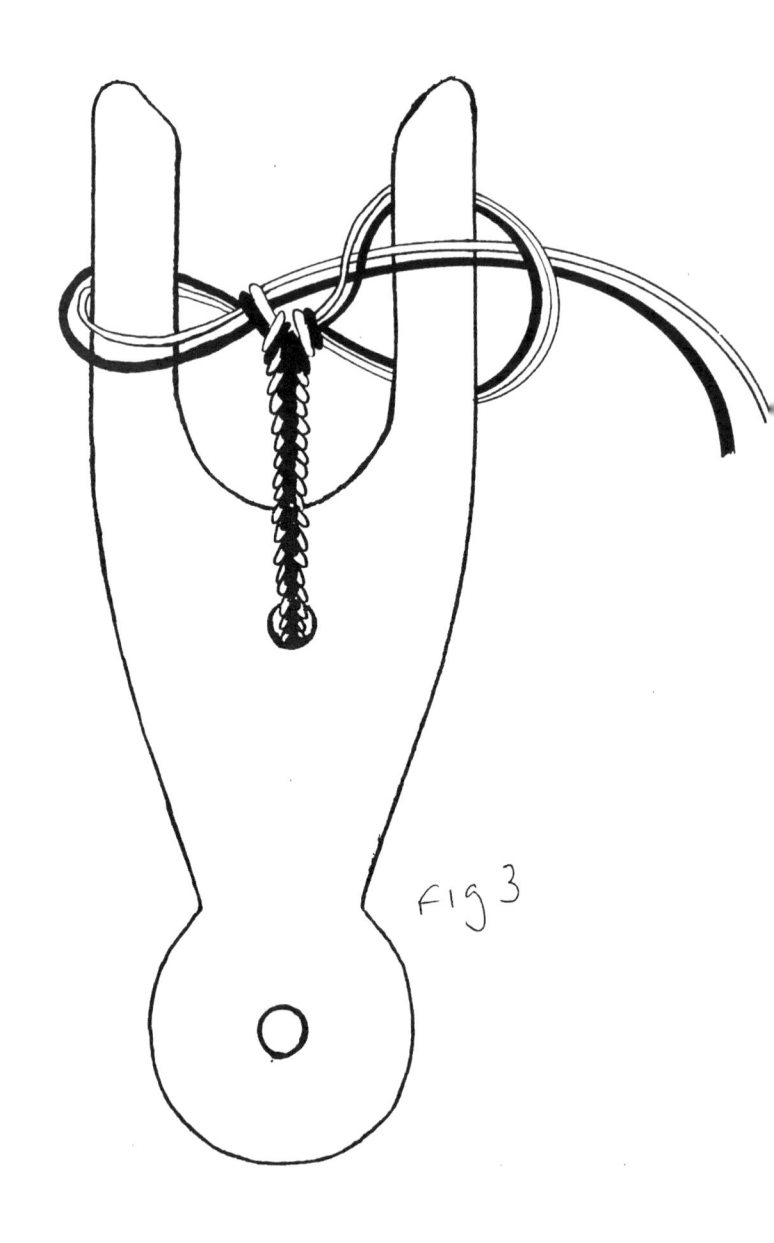

Cast over but do not snap shut.

- 12 -

Fig 4

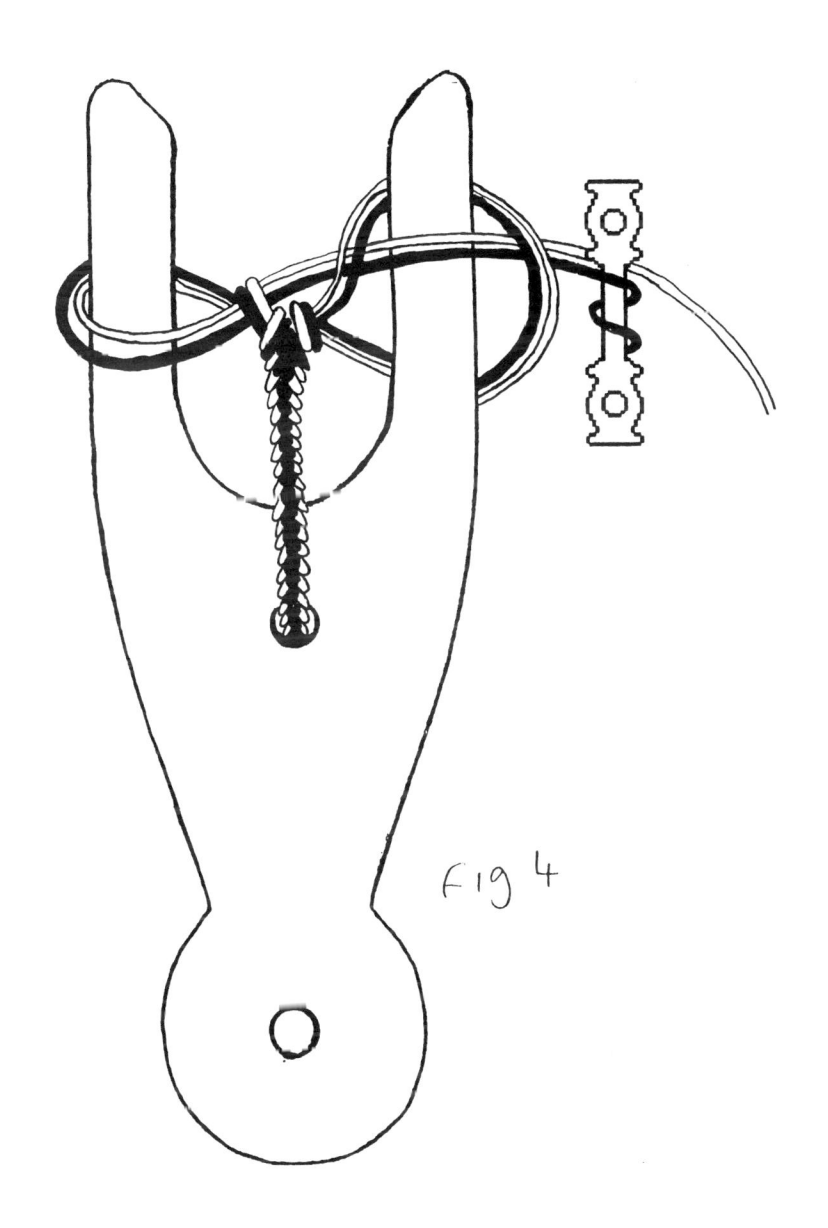

Wind up the excess B thread onto the bobbin bringing it to the edge of the Loop

Fig 5

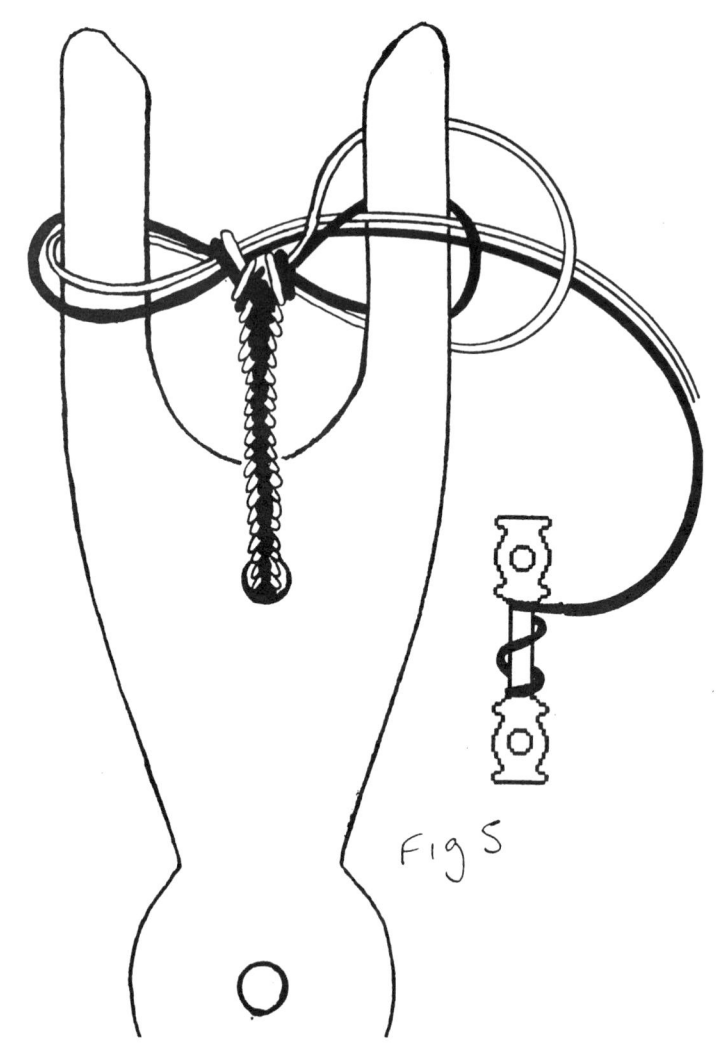

Holding onto the cord between the forks with the finger and thumb of the left hand, gently close the B loop by pulling on the bobbin, leaving the A loop exposed.

TIP If the A loop begins to close with the B loop ju tease it out with your fingers

Fig 6

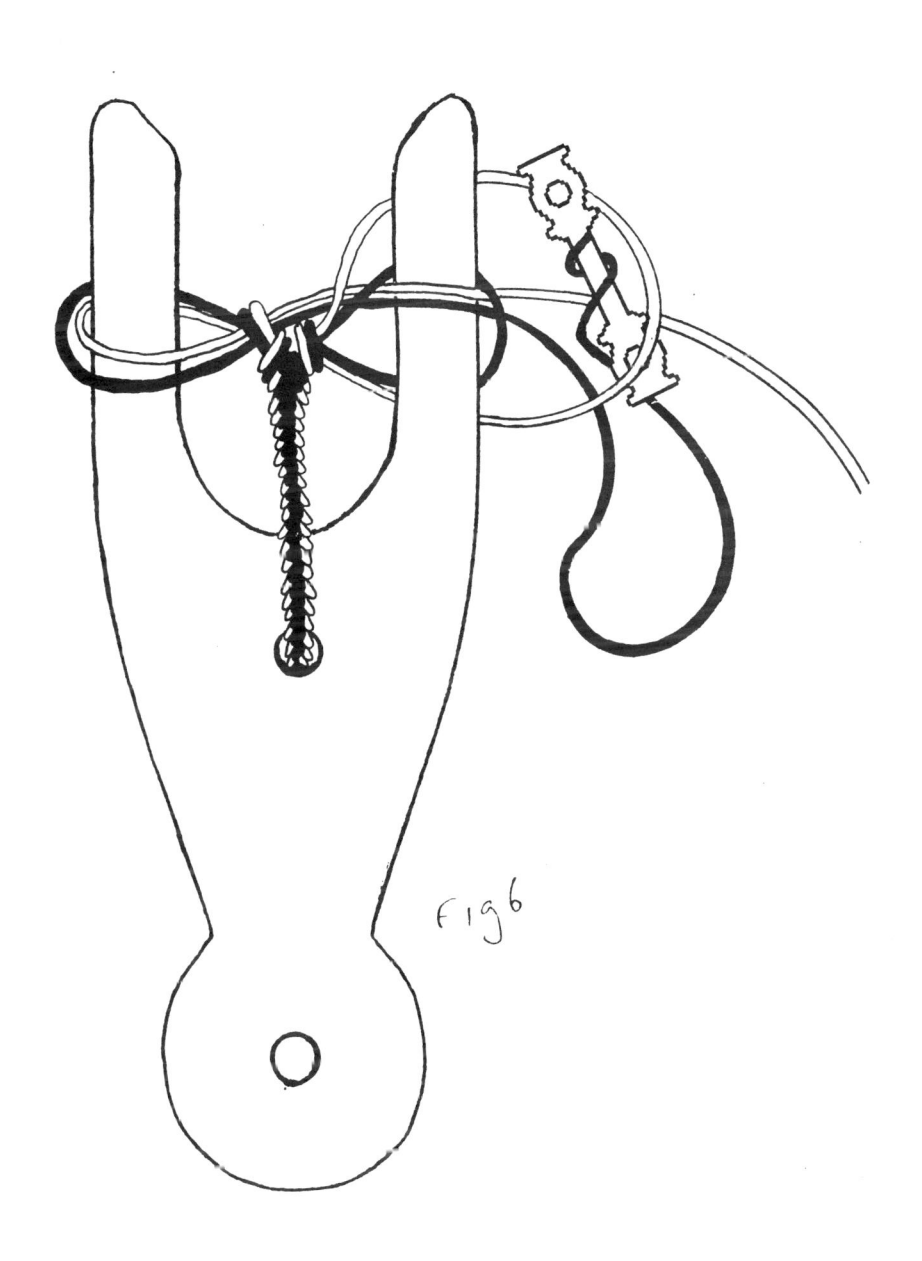

Pass the B bobbin from back to front through the exposed A Loop

Fig 7

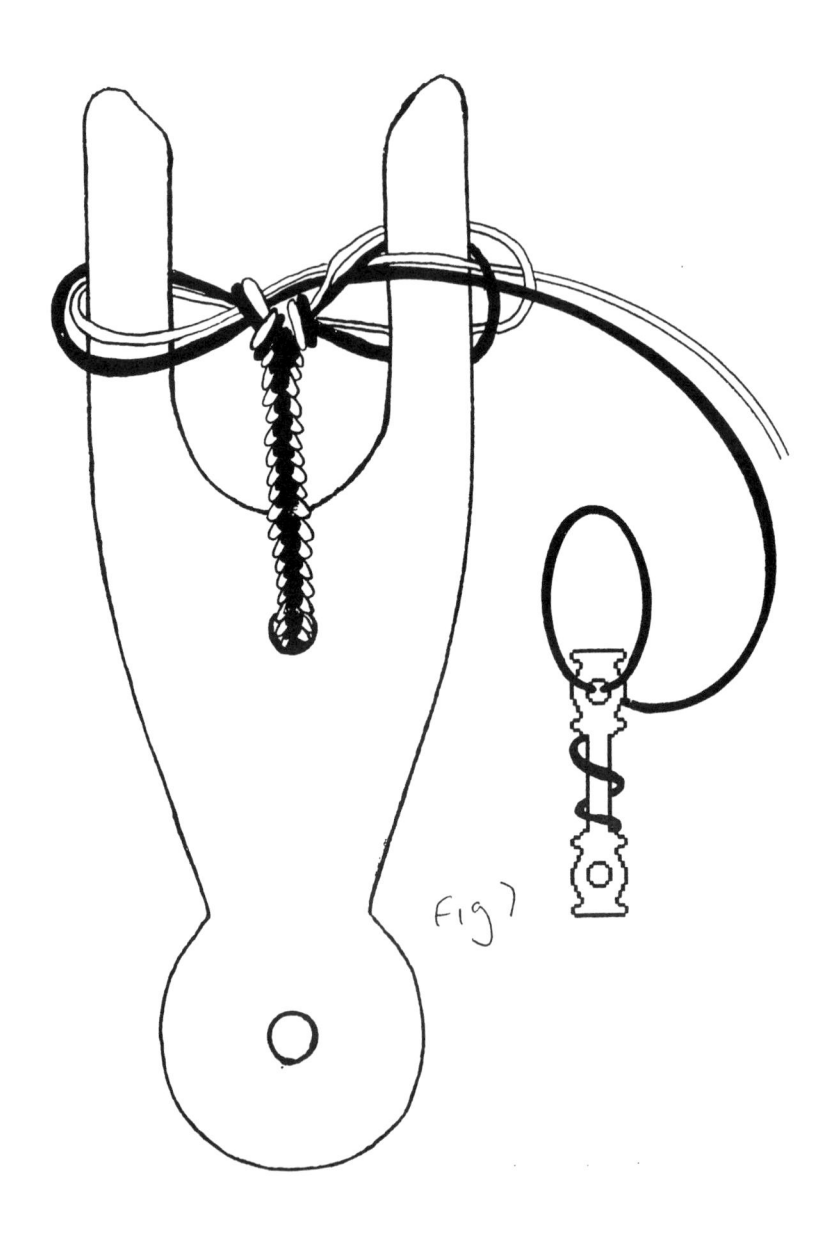

Close the A loop then thread lock the B bobbin (page 7) Turn the lucet

Fig 8

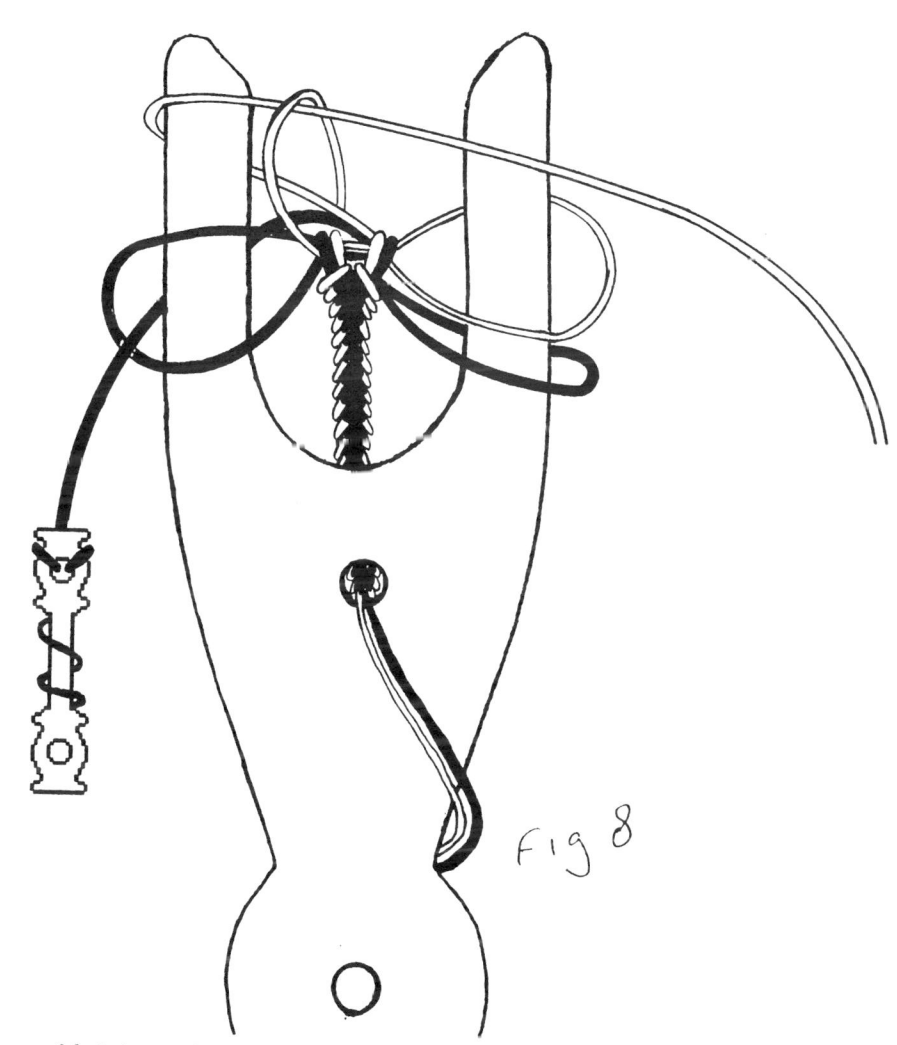

Holding the Lucet in the 'back' position (page 5) and keeping the B bobbin in the fingers, Lucet the A thread using the 'Back to front - front to back' method

TIP As you separate the threads use the finger and thumb of the Lucet hand to hold the B loops down, out of the way.

- 17 -

Fig 9

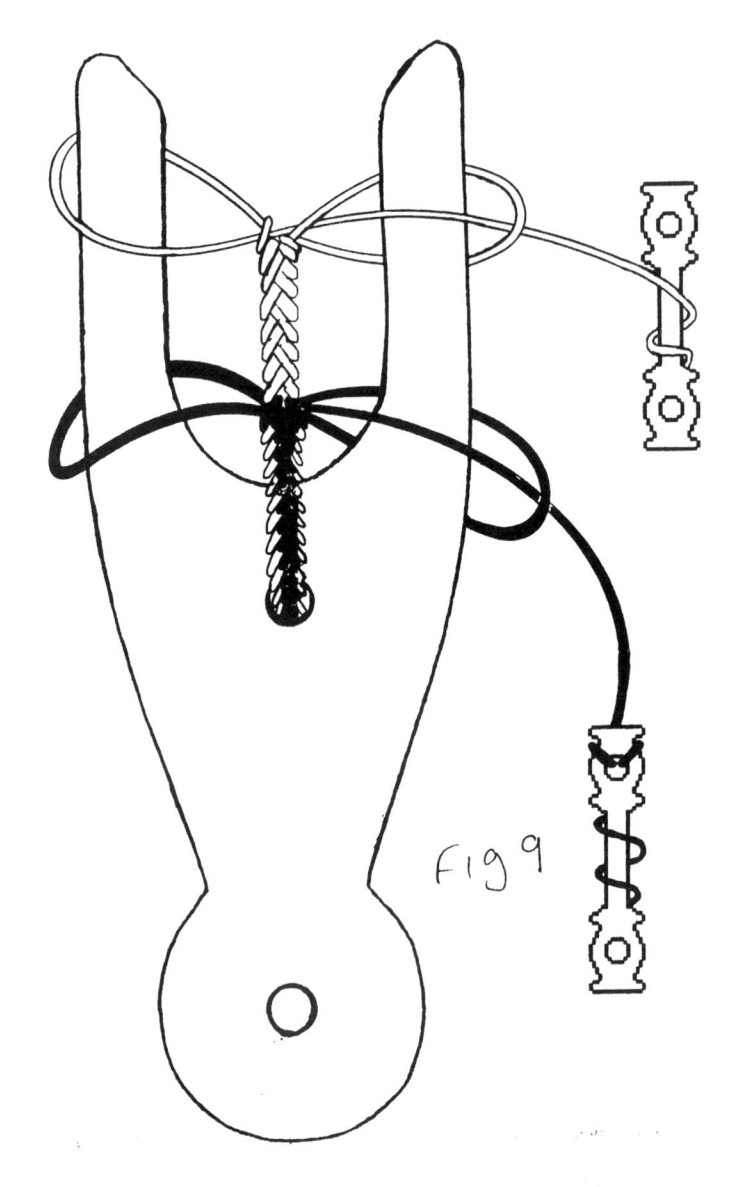

Having luceted twelve stitches of the A thread, wind up the excess thread onto the bobbin and bring it to about two inches of the fork.

Fig 10

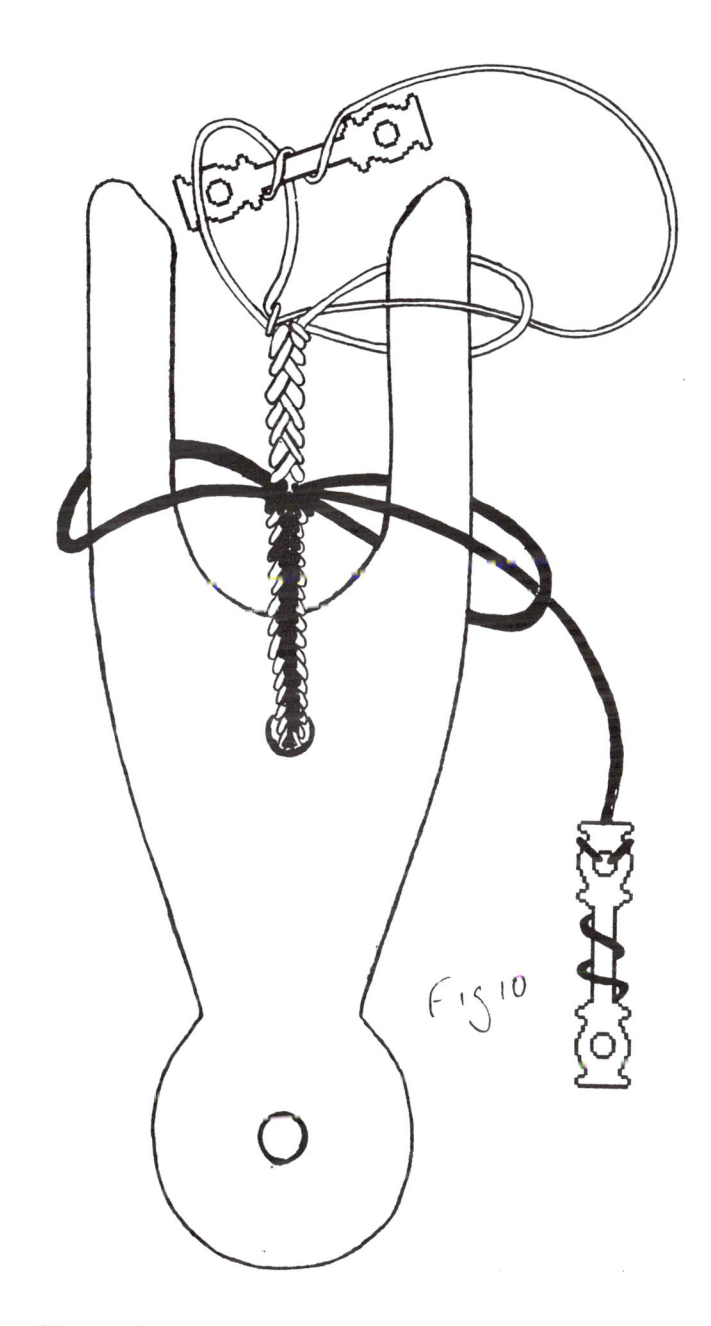

Using the bobbin, lift the Left Loop off the Left fork. (see Cradle Lock, page 8)

Fig 11

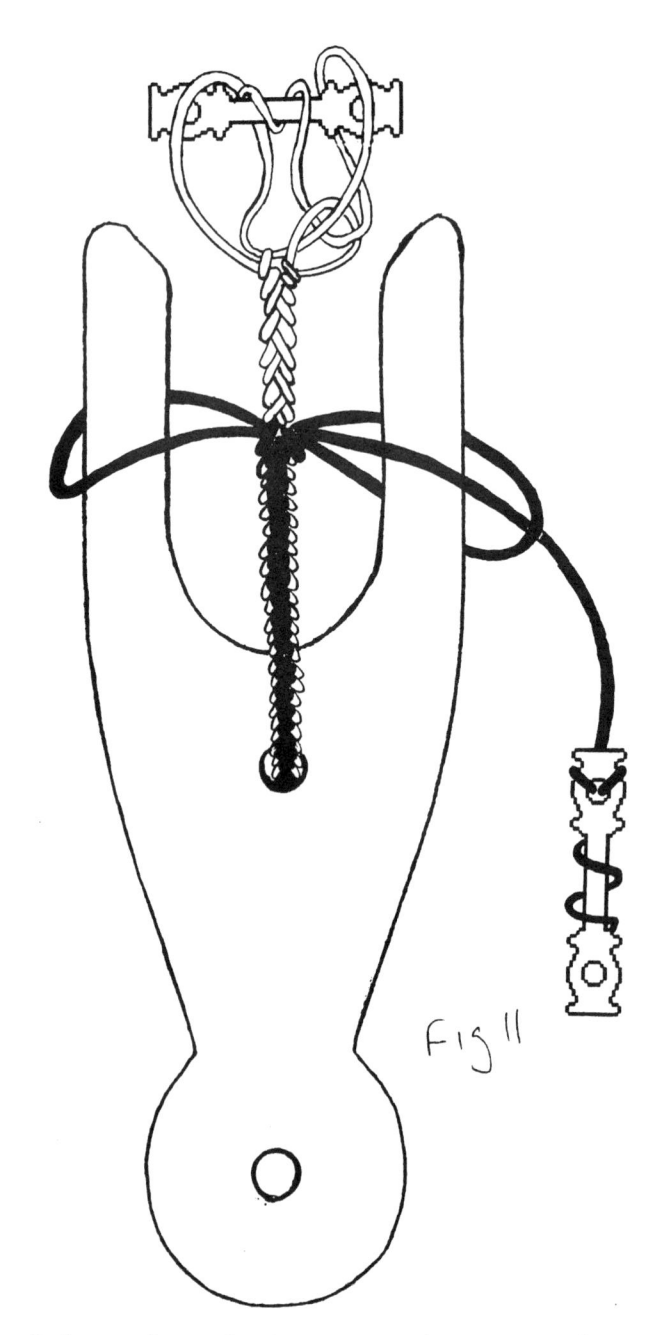

Pick up the right loop and place onto the right-hand-side of the bobbin.

Fig 12

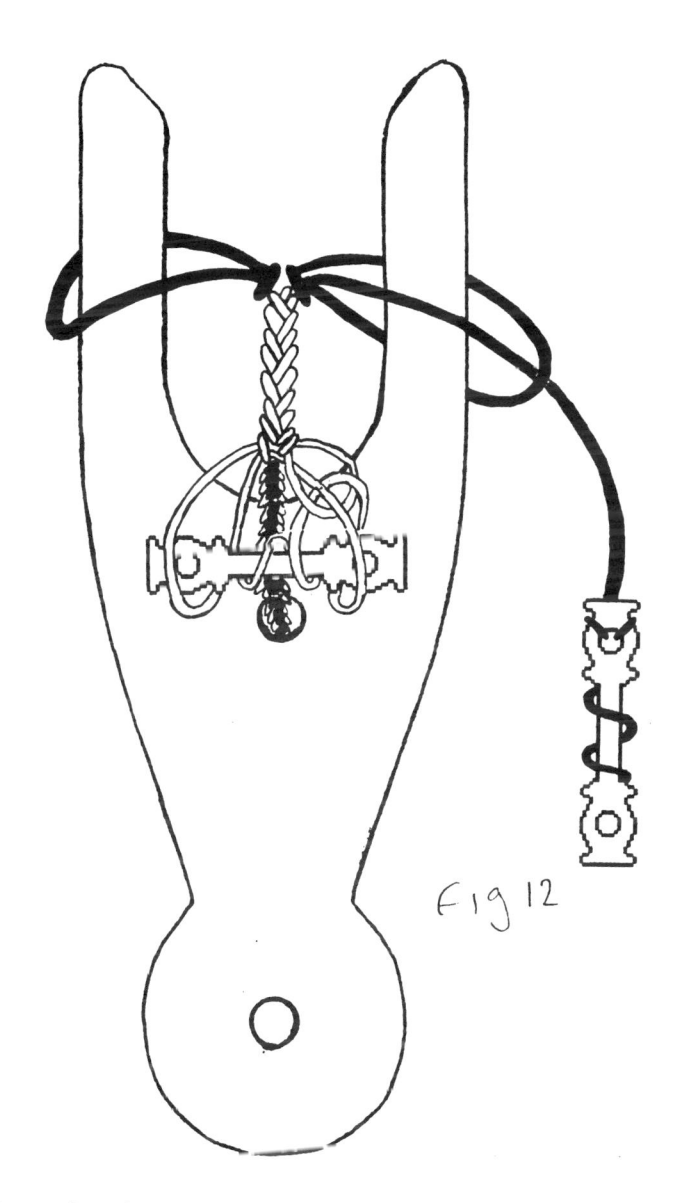

Pass the A bobbin through the forks and fold the cord at the join. Holding the bobbin in the 'front' position.

Fig 13

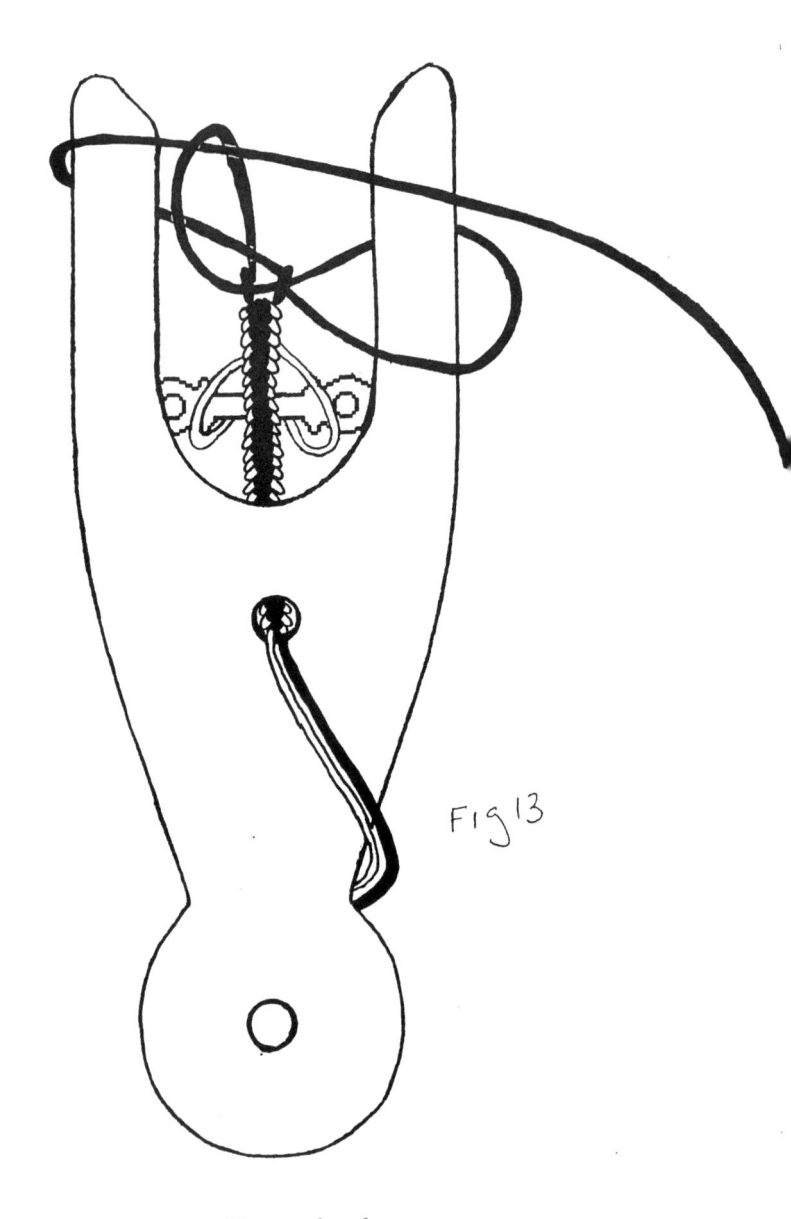

Turn the Lucet

Fig 14

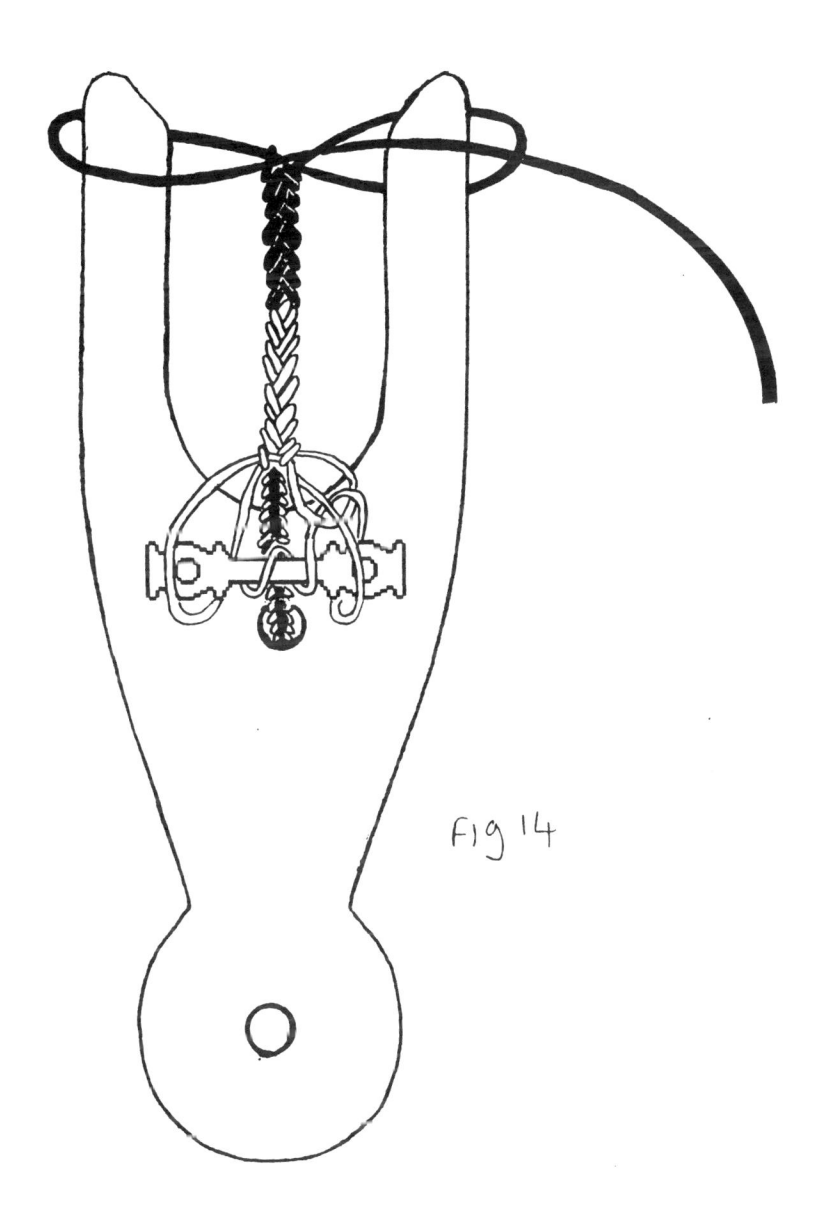

Lucet the B thread the same number of stitches as the A

FIG 15

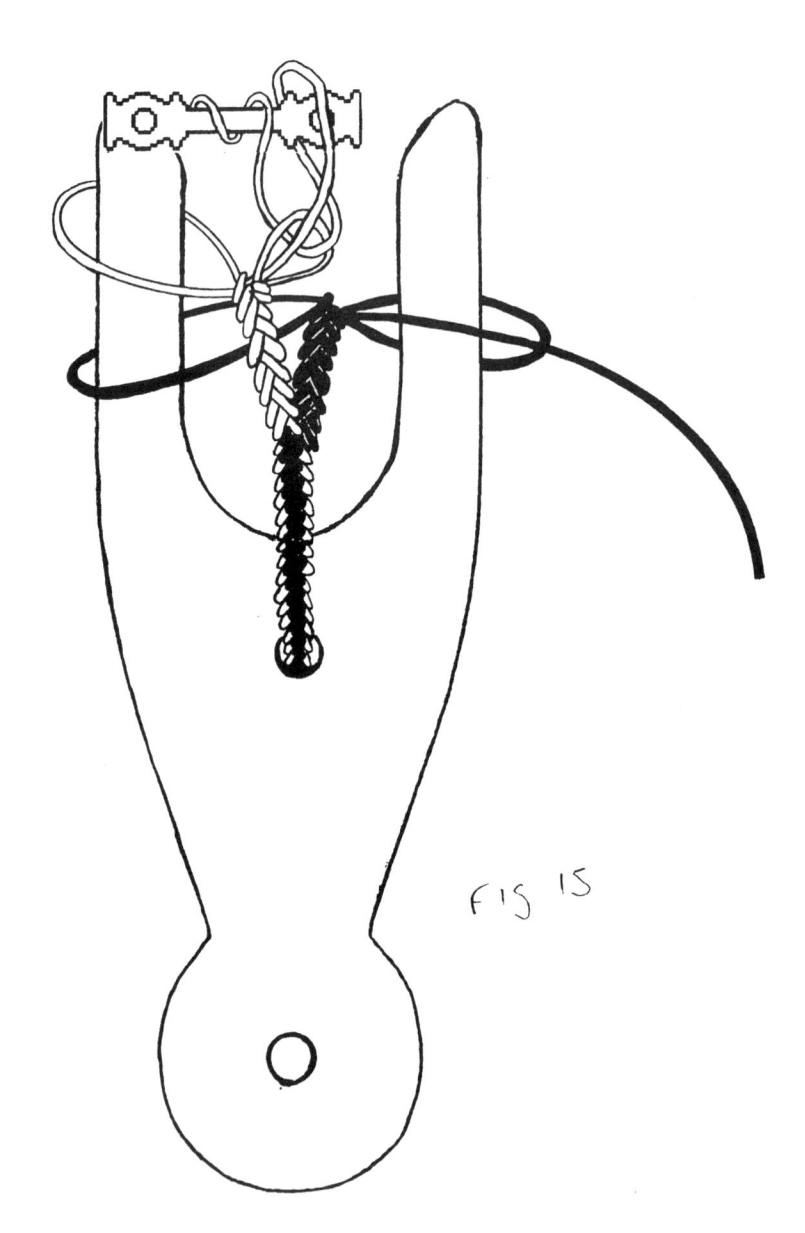

Bring the A bobbin back up, unlock the cradle lock (page 9) and drop the left loop back onto the left fork.

FIG 16

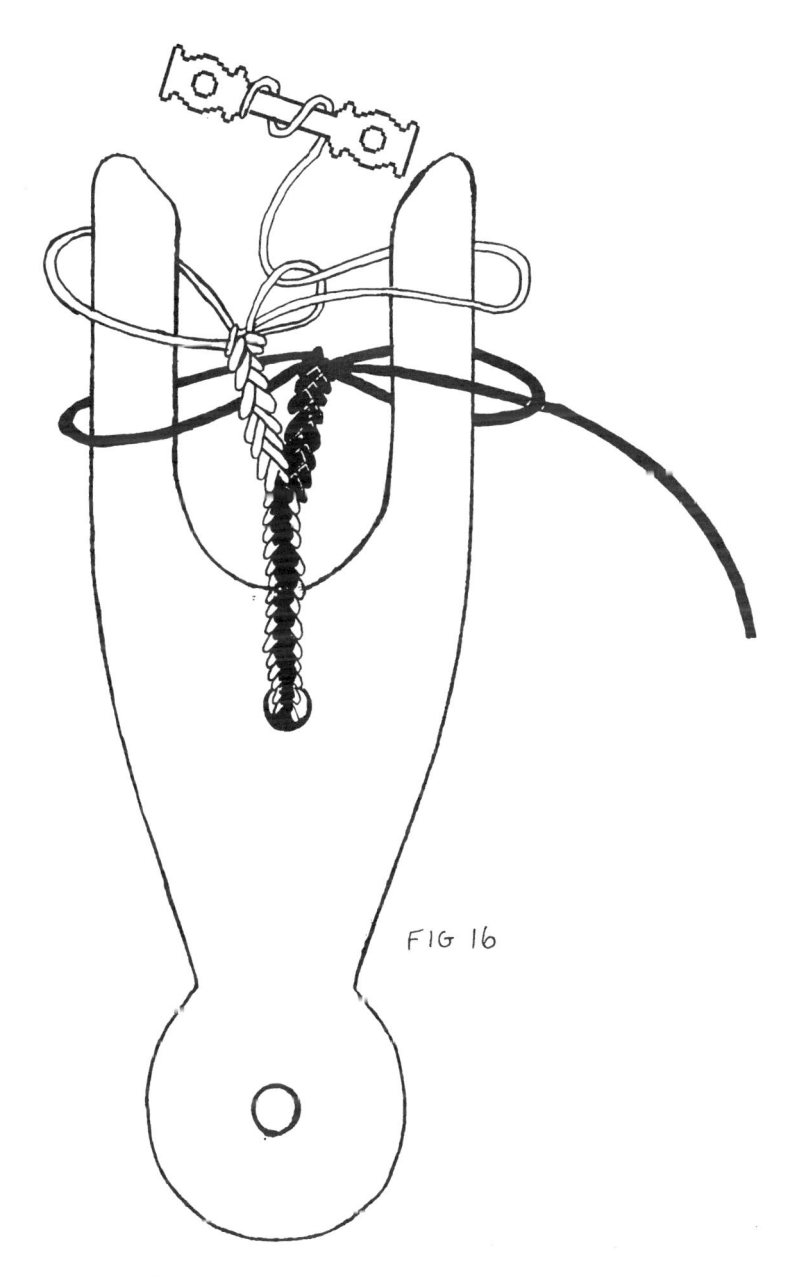

Drop the right loop back onto the right fork.

- 25 -

Fig 17

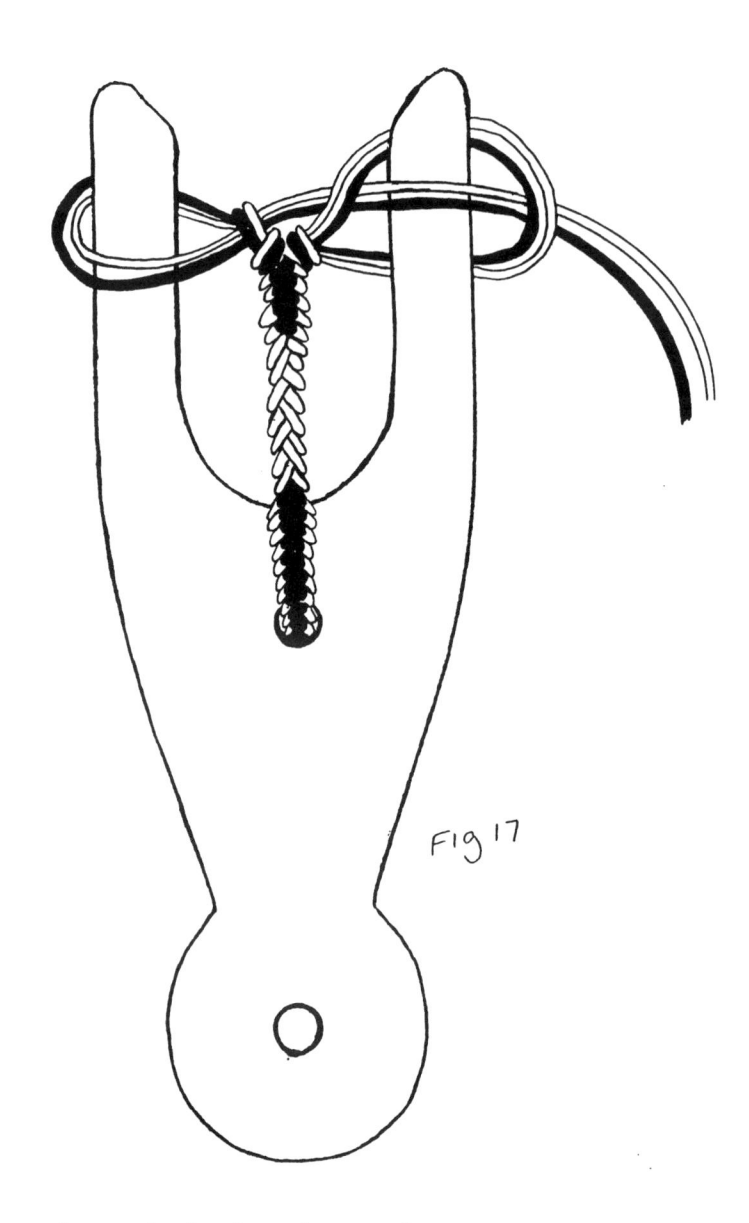

Lucet both threads together as one.

Crossover parallel

At the end of the Ziggy-Stitch when the threads are brought together again, Lucet for three stitches and on the fourth begin the Ziggy-Stitch again by pulling a larger loop off the back of the right fork, only this time close and thread lock the opposite thread.
Keep alternating each time you do a Ziggy-Stitch to produce a 'crossover parallel'.

Kiss-Cord

Take two bobbins of the same colour and Ziggy-Stich @ twelve stitches at the split and four to seal off and start another, keep making Ziggy-Stitches until the cord is of the required length then take two threads of a contrasting colour, Lucet them together to make a thick cord the same length then pass the thick cord in and out of the Ziggy-Stitches to make a 'Kiss-Cord'.